CW01673013

NIMSS

Advanced Vocabulary

for 11+, SATs and more...

Workbook 8: Q – R

Published & Designed By MASTERWELL LTD.
ISBN: 978-1-8380197-7-8
ADVANCED VOCABULARY WORKBOOK 8

Guide

Series Structure

This book is part 8 of a 10 book series.
The 10 books are split up as follows:

Workbook 1:	A – B	141	*Advanced Words*
Workbook 2:	C	129	*Advanced Words*
Workbook 3:	D	111	*Advanced Words*
Workbook 4:	E – F	124	*Advanced Words*
Workbook 5:	G – I	135	*Advanced Words*
Workbook 6:	J – N	128	*Advanced Words*
Workbook 7:	O – P	147	*Advanced Words*
Workbook 8:	**Q – R**	**89**	***Advanced Words***
Workbook 9:	S	141	*Advanced Words*
Workbook 10:	T – Z	150	*Advanced Words*

Add **1295** Advanced Words to you word bank with the

NIMSS Advanced Vocabulary Series.

Essential For:

- ✓ Eleven Plus (CEM/GL)
- ✓ The Transfer Test NI (AQE/GL)
- ✓ KS2 SATs (High Level)
- ✓ 12+ and 13+
- ✓ ISEB Common Entrance/Scholarship/Pre-Tests
- ✓ UKiset Tests
- ✓ The ISEE and SSAT (All Levels)
- ✓ Strengthening General Vocabulary

Elements of the Book

The **'Exercises'** in this book are designed to help students identify words of similar meanings, as well as understand the meanings of all these advanced words. As you will see, the synonyms provided in the bubble are in no way exhaustive, and will not in many cases have the exact same meaning as the key words. For example, happy, contended, thrilled and blissful are all synonyms, but all have subtly varying meanings, and are thus used in different contexts. Having said that, it is crucial for a child to recognise the positive connotation of all these words. The interactive structure of the exercises allows students to enhance and expand their word bank effectively.

At the end of each letter there are summary pages titled **'Answers & Revision Sheets'**. As suggested by the name, these are to be used to mark the exercises and for revision purposes.

There is also a list of **'Synonymless Words'** provided, which are words that do not have many synonyms. We believe that these words are important to be included in a child's word bank and have therefore been included as additional words.

We have also included tests at the end of each letter for you to **'Test Yourself'**. These are designed to help children refresh their memory with all the words they have recently covered.

Just before the Word Bank there are **'Crosswords'** for all the Synonymless Words. Their solutions are placed at the end of the Word Bank.

Right at the back of the book there is also a **'Word Bank'**.

How to use this book

Key Word 1 *word type A | word type B*	**Key Word 2** *word type: adjective/verb/noun*
A. first definition of key word 1. B. second definition of key word 1.	definition of key word 2.

In this bubble there will be up to 20 words.
These will all be similar words to either of
the two key words on the top of the page.
You must sort these into the table below.

Split similar words from the bubble above into their respective columns

	Key Word 1	**Key Word 2**
A	1.	1.
	2. Synonyms of	2.
	3. Key Word 1A	3.
	4. go in the first 5 rows	4.
	5.	5. Synonyms of
B	6.	6. Key Word 2 go in these 10 rows
	7. Synonyms of	7.
	8. Key Word 1B	8.
	9. go in the next 5 rows	9.
	10.	10.

Sample Exercise

Thrilled *adjective*	**Tense** *adjective | (verb) adjective*
extremely excited or pleased.	A. unable to relax because of nervousness or anxiety. B. (make a muscle) tight or rigid.

electrified overjoyed
elated stretch ecstatic
edgy happy
tight blissful
anxious
delighted taut
excited strain
lively stiff nervous
exhilarated
agitated restless

Split similar words from the bubble above into their respective columns

Thrilled	**Tense**	
1. *Happy*	1. *Nervous*	A
2. *Overjoyed*	2. *Anxious*	
3. *Ecstatic*	3. *Agitated*	
4. *Electrified*	4. *Edgy*	
5. *Elated*	5. *Restless*	
6. *Excited*	6. *Taut*	B
7. *Lively*	7. *Stiff*	
8. *Delighted*	8. *Tight*	
9. *Blissful*	9. *Strain*	
10. *Exhilarated*	10. *Stretch*	

Vocabulary can be overwhelming. Whether it be navigating through the endless verbal reasoning techniques in entrance examinations, grasping a passage of comprehension, or bringing your creative writing pieces to life, having a firm grip on vocabulary is essential.

This book is designed to help students familiarise themselves with the reams of vocabulary which they are expected to know.

Here at NIMSS, we firmly believe that after working through our Advanced Vocabulary series, students will be more confident undertaking any exercise which involves vocabulary.

A message from the makers

NIMSS

Contents

Q

Exercises 9

Synonymless Words 12

Answers & Revision Sheet 13

Test Yourself 14

Answers 16

R

Exercises 18

Synonymless Words 53

Answers & Revision Sheet 54

Test Yourself 62

Answers 68

Crossword 69

Word Bank 70

Q

NIMSS

1. Quintessential *adjective*	2. Quaint *adjective*
representing the most perfect or typical example of a quality or class.	attractively unusual or old-fashioned.

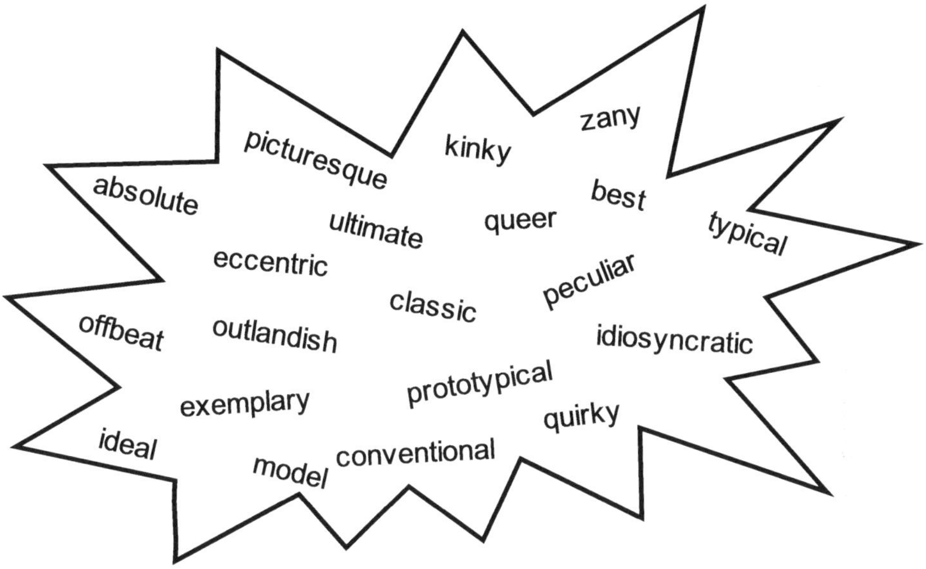

Split similar words from the bubble above into their respective columns

Quintessential	Quaint
1.	1.
2.	2.
3.	3.
4.	4.
5.	5.
6.	6.
7.	7.
8.	8.
9.	9.
10.	10.

3. Quay *noun*	**4. Quandary** *noun*
a stone or metal platform lying alongside or projecting into water for loading and unloading ships.	a state of perplexity or uncertainty over what to do in a difficult situation.

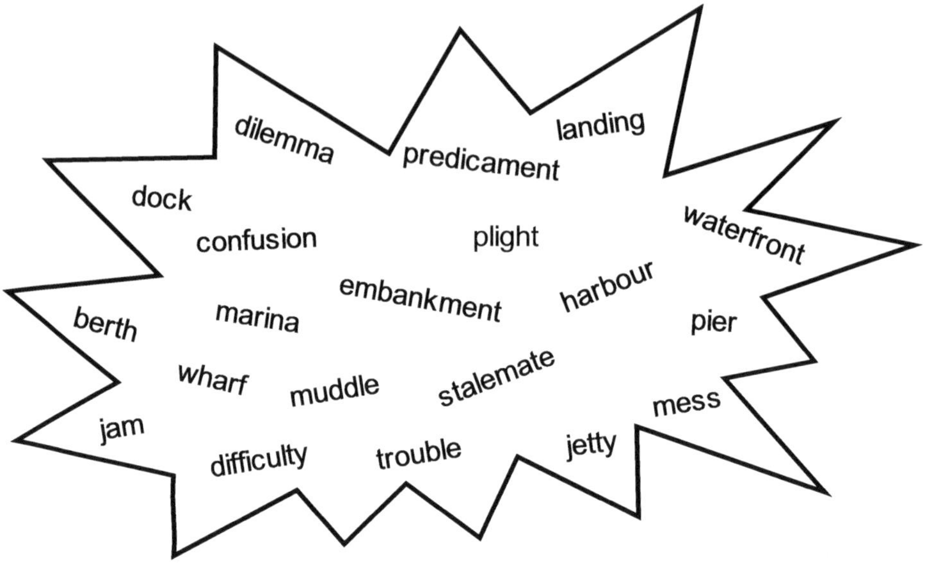

Split similar words from the bubble above into their respective columns

Quay	**Quandary**
1.	1.
2.	2.
3.	3.
4.	4.
5.	5.
6.	6.
7.	7.
8.	8.
9.	9.
10.	10.

5. Quell *verb*	**6. Quail** *verb*
put an end to (a rebellion or other disorder), typically by the use of force; suppress (a feeling).	feel or show fear or apprehension. (also a small game bird)

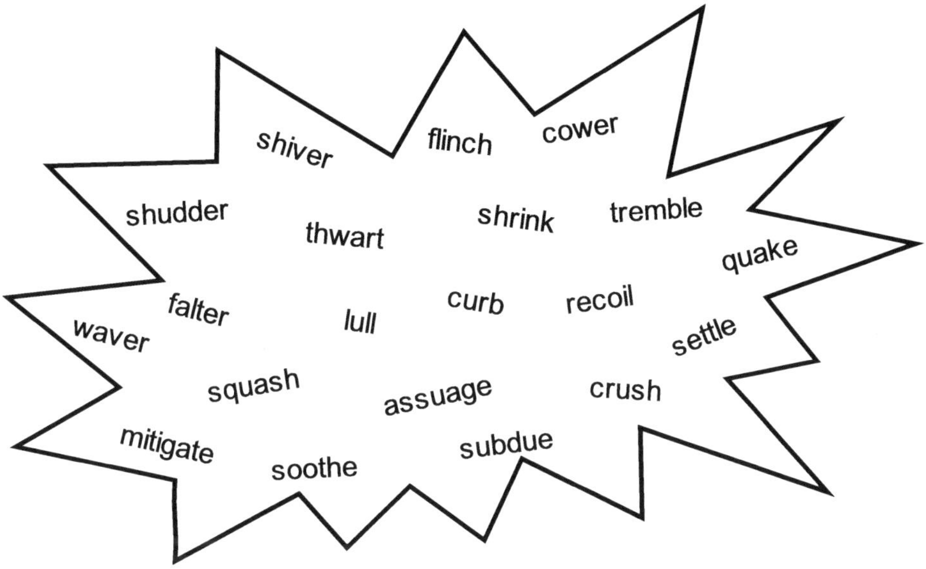

Split similar words from the bubble above into their respective columns

<u>Quell</u>	**<u>Quail</u>**
1.	1.
2.	2.
3.	3.
4.	4.
5.	5.
6.	6.
7.	7.
8.	8.
9.	9.
10.	10.

Synonymless Words

These are words with few or no synonyms.

Word		Definition
7.	Quiche	a baked flan or tart with a savoury filling thickened with eggs, usually eaten cold.
8.	Quid pro quo	a favour or advantage granted in return for something.
9.	Quince	a hard, acid pear-shaped fruit used in preserves or as flavouring.
10.	Quartz	a hard mineral consisting of silica typically occurring as colourless prisms.

A Crossword for Synonymless Words can be found near the end of this book.

Answers & Revision Sheets Q

1. Quintessential	2. Quaint	3. Quay
• Typical • Classic • Prototypical • Conventional • Ideal • Exemplary • Ultimate • Model • Absolute • Best	• Eccentric • Idiosyncratic • Outlandish • Peculiar • Offbeat • Zany • Kinky • Picturesque • Quirky • Queer	• Dock • Harbour • Pier • Wharf • Marina • Jetty • Embankment • Landing • Birth • Waterfront
4. Quandary	**5. Quell**	**6. Quail**
• Dilemma • Predicament • Plight • Trouble • Muddle • Stalemate • Difficulty • Jam • Confusion • Mess	• Thwart • Curb • Crush • Squash • Subdue • Soothe • Settle • Lull • Assuage • Mitigate	• Cower • Waver • Falter • Flinch • Recoil • Shudder • Tremble • Quake • Shiver • Shrink

Test Yourself: Q

Fill in the gaps! This will help refresh your memory of all the words you have just covered. The first one is done for you.

1. Waterfront	Q U A Y
2. Exemplary	Q _ I N _ _ S S _ N _ I _ L
3. Dilemma	Q _ _ N D _ R _
4. Peculiar	Q _ _ I N _
5. Suppress	Q _ _ L L
6. Flinch	Q _ A _ _

Please turn over for Answers

Answers

1. Quay
2. Quintessential
3. Quandary
4. Quaint
5. Quell
6. Quail

R

NIMSS

1. Rapt *adjective*	2. Resolute *adjective*
completely fascinated or absorbed by what one is seeing or hearing.	admirably purposeful, determined, and unwavering.

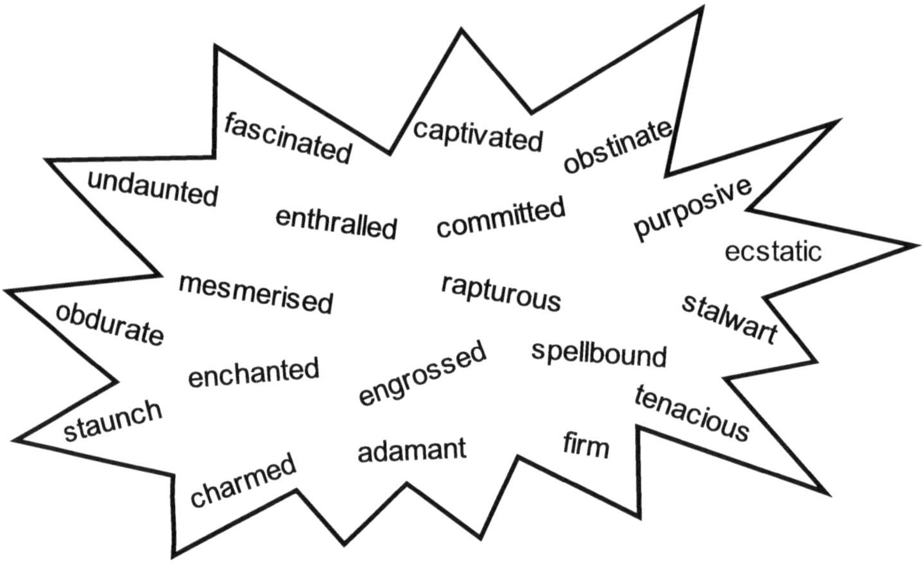

Split similar words from the bubble above into their respective columns

Rapt	**Resolute**
1.	1.
2.	2.
3.	3.
4.	4.
5.	5.
6.	6.
7.	7.
8.	8.
9.	9.
10.	10.

3. Rambling *adjective*	4. Rudimentary *adjective*
(of writing or speech) lengthy and confused; (of a building or path) spreading or winding irregularly	involving or limited to basic principles; relating to an immature, undeveloped, or basic form.

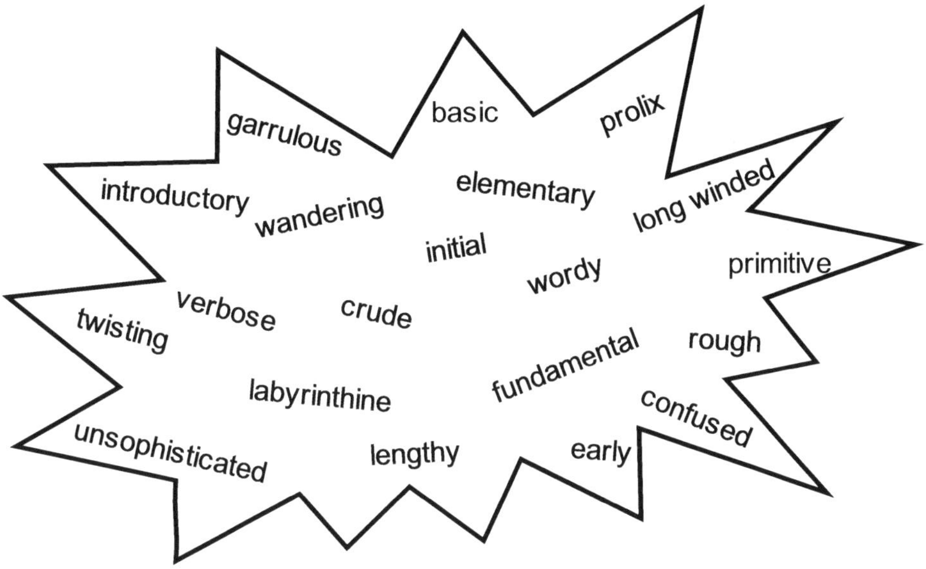

Split similar words from the bubble above into their respective columns

Rambling	**Rudimentary**
1.	1.
2.	2.
3.	3.
4.	4.
5.	5.
6.	6.
7.	7.
8.	8.
9.	9.
10.	10.

5. Ramshackle *adjective*	**6. Rancid** *adjective*
(especially of a house or vehicle) in a state of severe disrepair.	(of foods containing fat or oil) smelling or tasting unpleasant as a result of being old and stale.

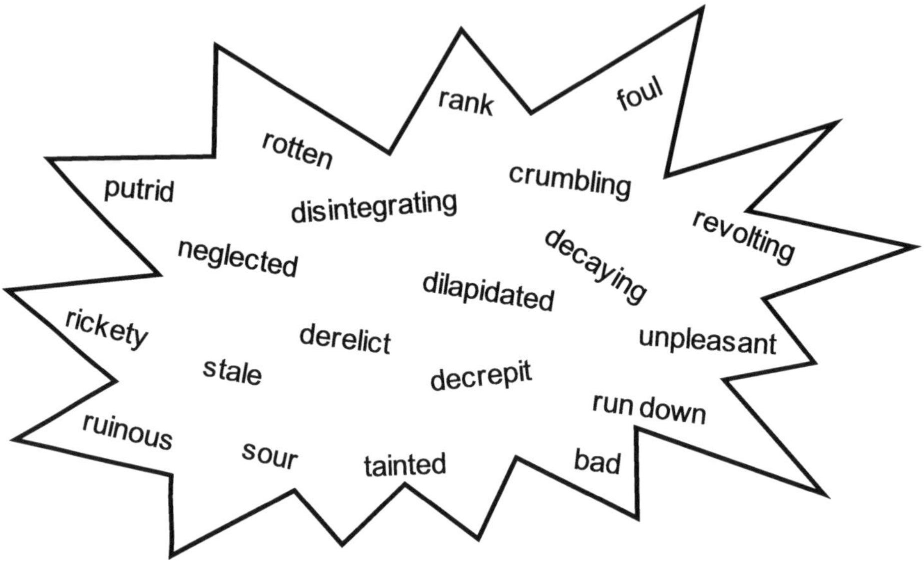

Split similar words from the bubble above into their respective columns

Ramshackle	**Rancid**
1.	1.
2.	2.
3.	3.
4.	4.
5.	5.
6.	6.
7.	7.
8.	8.
9.	9.
10.	10.

7. Recluse *noun*	**8. Renegade** *(adjective) noun*
a person who lives a solitary life and tends to avoid other people.	(characteristic of) a person who deserts and betrays an organization, country, or set of principles.

hermit, nun, monk, mutinous, traitorous, rebellious, disloyal, solitary, traitor, rebel, defector, loner, introvert, turncoat, ascetic, treacherous, deserter

Split similar words from the bubble above into their respective columns

Recluse	**Renegade**
1.	1.
2.	2.
3.	3.
4.	4.
5.	5.
6.	6.
7.	7.
8.	8.
9.	9.
10.	10.

9. Rebate *noun*	10. Rubble *noun*
a partial refund to someone who has paid too much for tax, rent, or a utility.	waste or rough fragments of stone, concrete, etc., especially as the debris from the demolition of buildings.

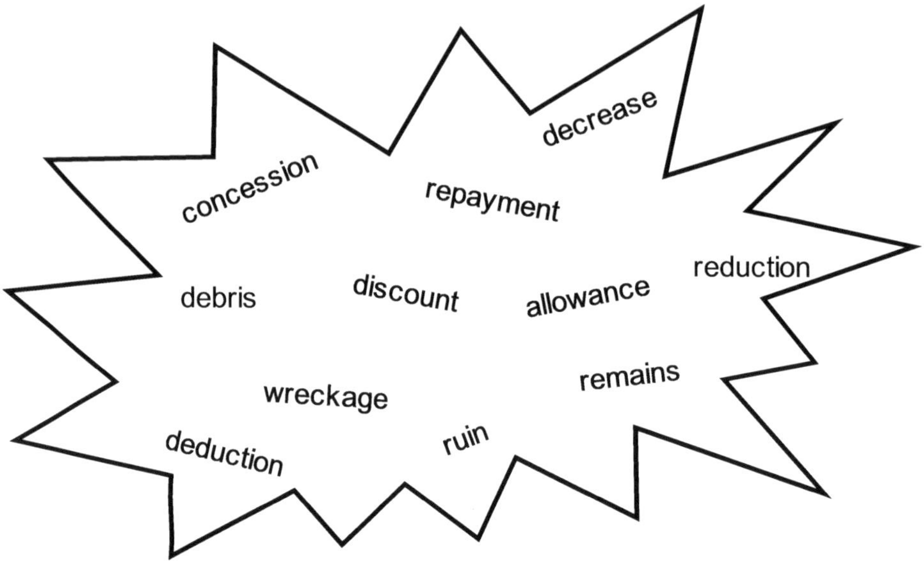

Split similar words from the bubble above into their respective columns

Rebate	**Rubble**
1.	1.
2.	2.
3.	3.
4.	4.
5.	5.
6.	6.
7.	7.
8.	8.
9.	9.
10.	10.

11. Reel *verb*	**12. Reproach** *(verb) noun*
lose balance and stagger violently. (also a Scottish dance and cylindrical tool for string or wire)	(give someone) the expression of disapproval or disappointment.

rebuke lurch
berate
stagger wobble castigate
roll censure swerve
totter admonition
rock upbraid reproof
reprimand
chide stumble
waver chastise

Split similar words from the bubble above into their respective columns

Reel	**Reproach**
1.	1.
2.	2.
3.	3.
4.	4.
5.	5.
6.	6.
7.	7.
8.	8.
9.	9.
10.	10.

13. Raze *verb*	**14. Replenish** *verb*
completely destroy (a building, town, or other settlement).	fill something up again.

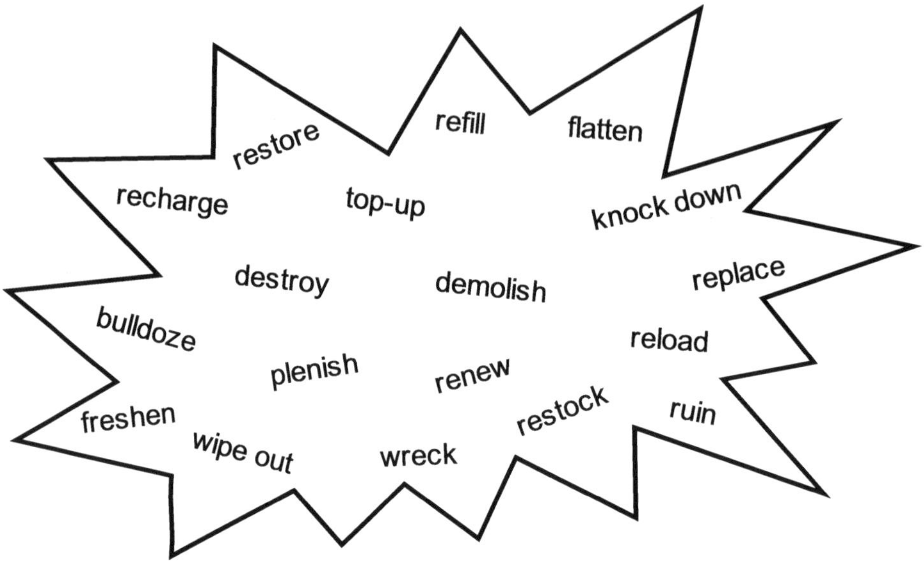

Split similar words from the bubble above into their respective columns

Rave	**Replenish**
1.	1.
2.	2.
3.	3.
4.	4.
5.	5.
6.	6.
7.	7.
8.	8.
9.	9.
10.	10.

15. Repudiate *verb*	**16. Rave** *verb | verb | noun*
refuse to accept; deny the truth or validity of.	A. talk incoherently in a angry way. B. speak or write about someone or something with great admiration. C. a lively party.

frolic
disavow
ramble
babble
deny
disclaim
contradict
maunder
negate
festivity
extol
desert
abandon
reject
refute
rant
eulogise
acclaim
renounce
celebration

Split similar words from the bubble above into their respective columns

Repudiate	**Rave**	
1.	1.	A
2.	2.	
3.	3.	
4.	4.	
5.	5.	
6.	6.	
7.	7.	
8.	8.	B
9.	9.	
10.	10.	

17. Relinquish *verb*	18. Recede *verb*
voluntarily cease to keep or claim; give up.	go or move back or further away from a previous position; gradually diminish.

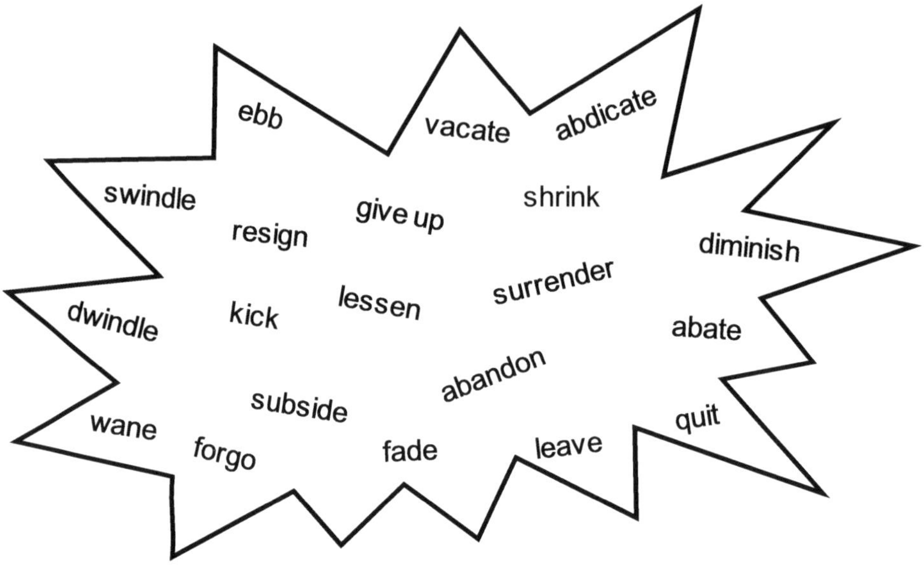

Split similar words from the bubble above into their respective columns

Relinquish	**Recede**
1.	1.
2.	2.
3.	3.
4.	4.
5.	5.
6.	6.
7.	7.
8.	8.
9.	9.
10.	10.

19. Revel *verb*	20. Reimburse *verb*
enjoy oneself in a lively and noisy way; get great pleasure from (a situation or experience).	repay (a sum of money)

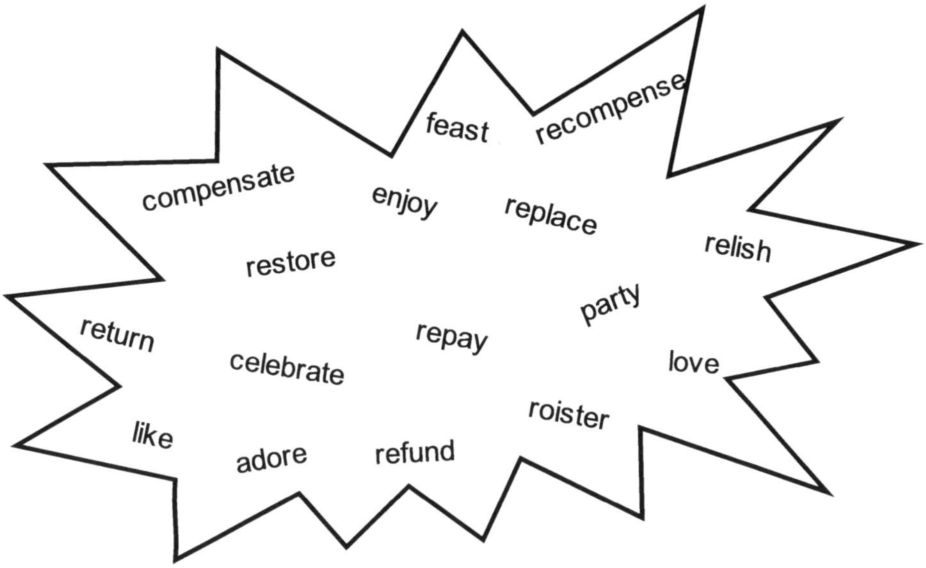

Split similar words from the bubble above into their respective columns

Revel	**Reimburse**
1.	1.
2.	2.
3.	3.
4.	4.
5.	5.
6.	6.
7.	7.
8.	8.
9.	9.
10.	10.

21. Reek *(verb) noun*	**22. Ravage** *verb*
(have a) smell strongly and unpleasantly.	cause severe and extensive damage to.

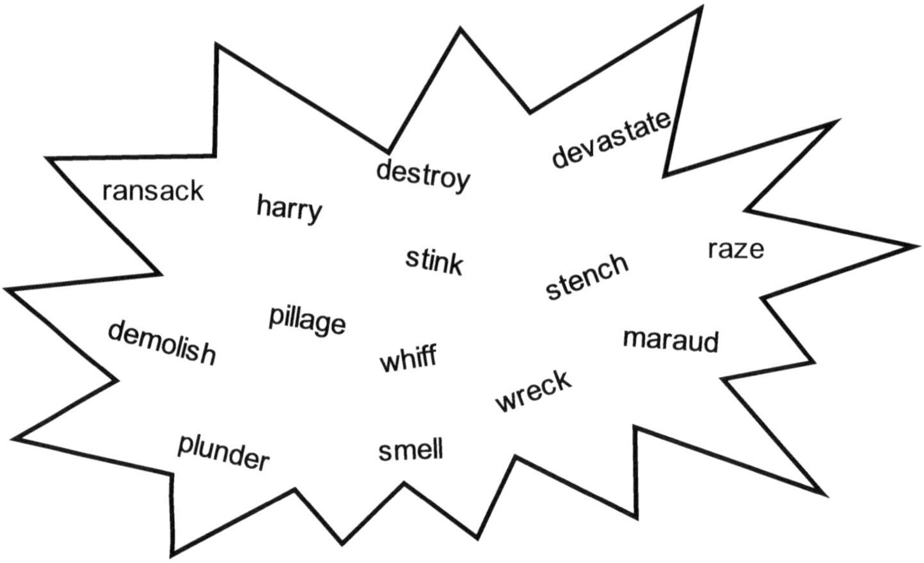

Split similar words from the bubble above into their respective columns

Reek	**Ravage**
1.	1.
2.	2.
3.	3.
4.	4.
5.	5.
6.	6.
7.	7.
8.	8.
9.	9.
10.	10.

23. Recurrent adjective	**24. Reticent** *adjective*
occurring often or repeatedly. turning back so as to reverse direction.	not revealing one's thoughts or feelings readily.

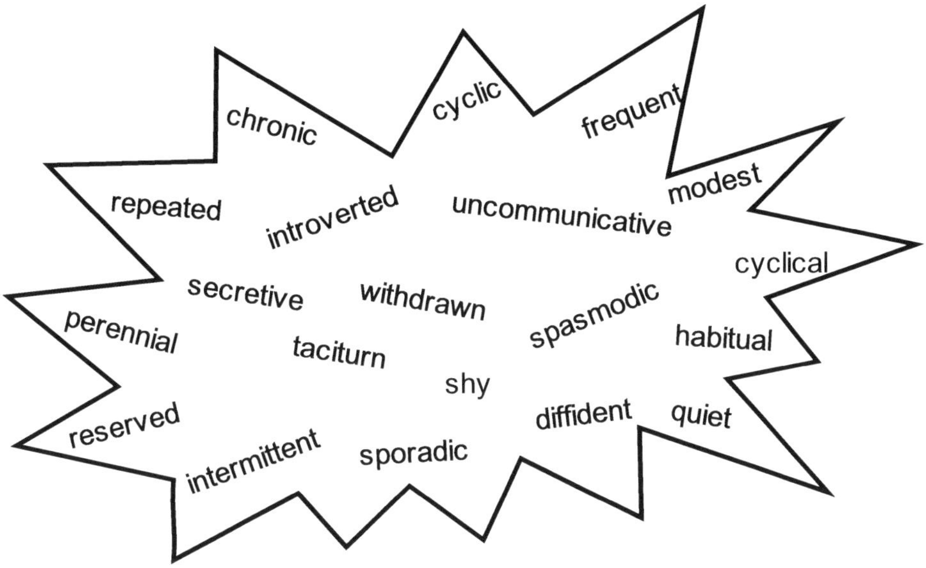

Split similar words from the bubble above into their respective columns

Recurrent	**Reticent**
1.	1.
2.	2.
3.	3.
4.	4.
5.	5.
6.	6.
7.	7.
8.	8.
9.	9.
10.	10.

25. Rife *adjective*	26. Reclusive *adjective*
(especially of something undesirable) of common occurrence; full of.	avoiding the company of other people.

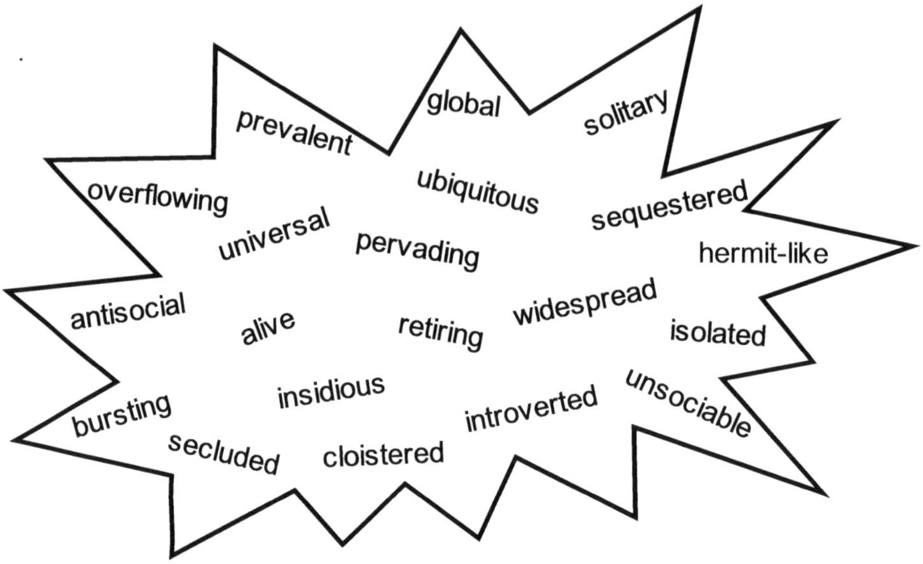

Split similar words from the bubble above into their respective columns

Rife	**Reclusive**
1.	1.
2.	2.
3.	3.
4.	4.
5.	5.
6.	6.
7.	7.
8.	8.
9.	9.
10.	10.

27. Rile *verb*	**28. Revile** *verb*
make (someone) annoyed or irritated.	criticize in an abusive or angrily insulting manner.

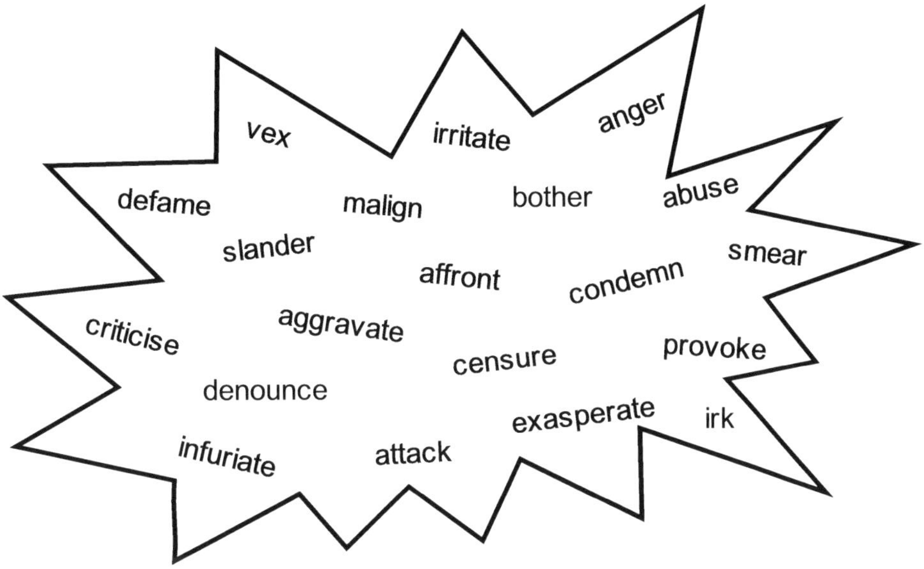

Split similar words from the bubble above into their respective columns

Rile	**Revile**
1.	1.
2.	2.
3.	3.
4.	4.
5.	5.
6.	6.
7.	7.
8.	8.
9.	9.
10.	10.

29. Retort *(verb) noun*	30. Relish *noun & (verb) | noun*
(give) a sharp, angry, or witty reply.	A. great enjoyment (enjoy greatly). B. a piquant sauce or pickle eaten with plain food to add flavour.

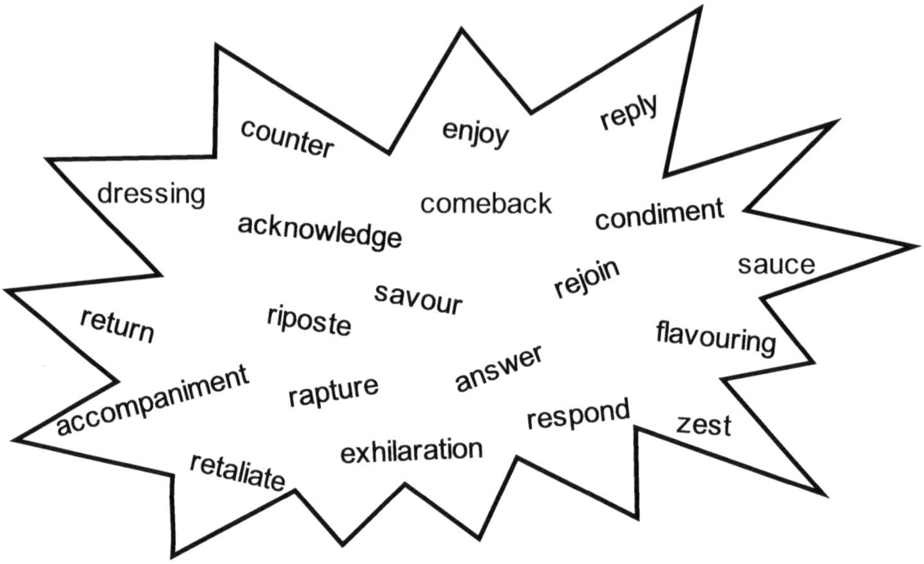

Split similar words from the bubble above into their respective columns

Retort	**Relish**	
1.	1.	A
2.	2.	
3.	3.	
4.	4.	
5.	5.	
6.	6.	B
7.	7.	
8.	8.	
9.	9.	
10.	10.	

31. Ragged *adjective*	**32. Ravishing** *adjective*
(of cloth or clothes) old and torn; having an irregular or uneven surface, edge, or outline.	delightful.

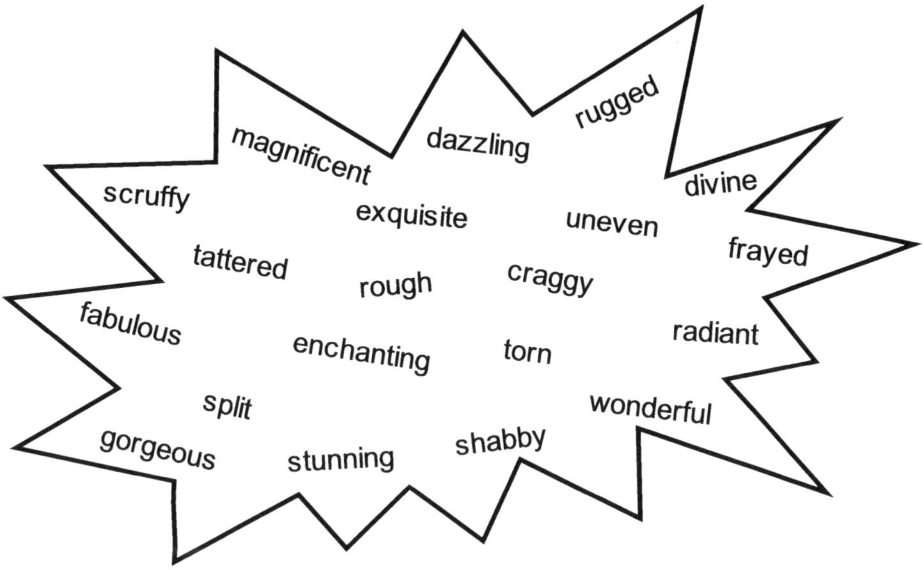

Split similar words from the bubble above into their respective columns

<u>**Ragged**</u>	<u>**Ravishing**</u>
1.	1.
2.	2.
3.	3.
4.	4.
5.	5.
6.	6.
7.	7.
8.	8.
9.	9.
10.	10.

33. Raiment *noun*	34. Rapport *noun*
clothing.	a close and harmonious relationship.

dress
vestment
link
garb
costume
clothing
accord
clothes
harmony
sympathy
apparel
empathy
garments
outfit
affinity
bond
attire

Split similar words from the bubble above into their respective columns

Raiment	**Rapport**
1.	1.
2.	2.
3.	3.
4.	4.
5.	5.
6.	6.
7.	7.
8.	8.
9.	9.
10.	10.

35. Rancour *noun*	**36. Recess** *noun | noun*
bitterness or resentfulness, especially when long standing.	A. a space created by building part of a wall further back from the rest. B. a temporary break in proceedings.

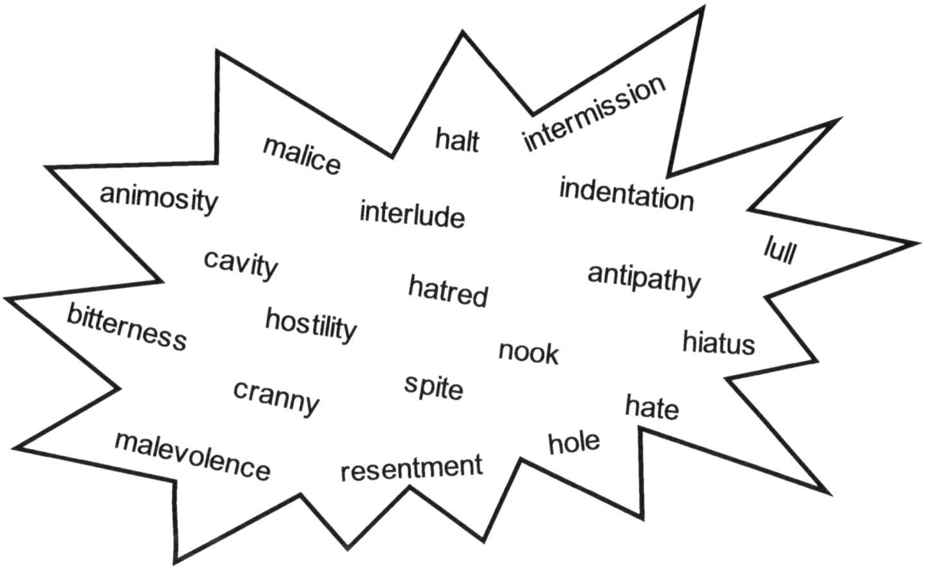

Split similar words from the bubble above into their respective columns

Rancour	**Recess**	
1.	1.	A
2.	2.	
3.	3.	
4.	4.	
5.	5.	
6.	6.	B
7.	7.	
8.	8.	
9.	9.	
10.	10.	

37. Ransack *verb*	38. Rasp *(verb) noun*
go through (a place) stealing things and causing damage.	(make) a harsh, grating noise; (scrape something with) a metal tool or file.

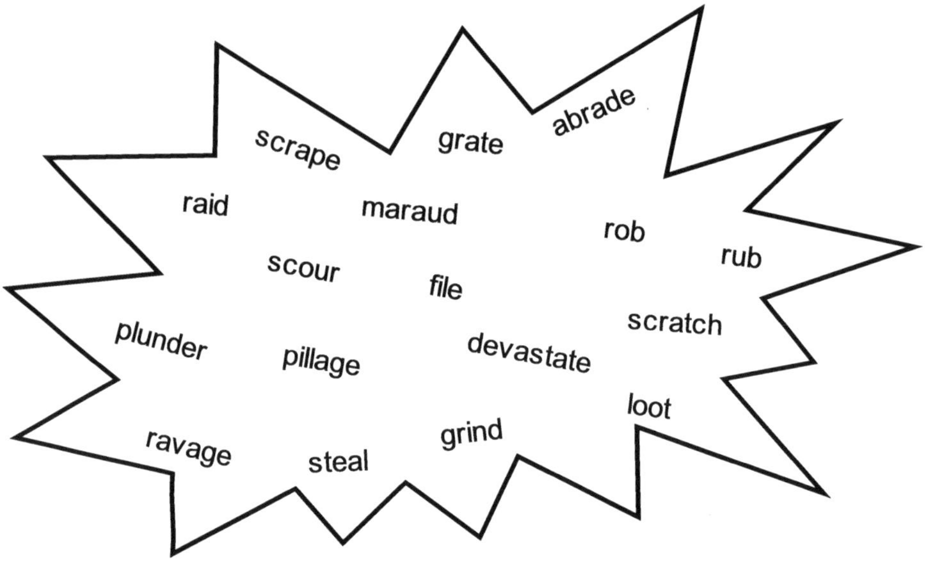

Split similar words from the bubble above into their respective columns

Ransack	**Rasp**
1.	1.
2.	2.
3.	3.
4.	4.
5.	5.
6.	6.
7.	7.
8.	8.
9.	9.
10.	10.

39. Rapturous *adjective*	40. Raucous *adjective*
characterized by, feeling, or expressing great pleasure or enthusiasm.	making or constituting a disturbingly harsh and loud noise.

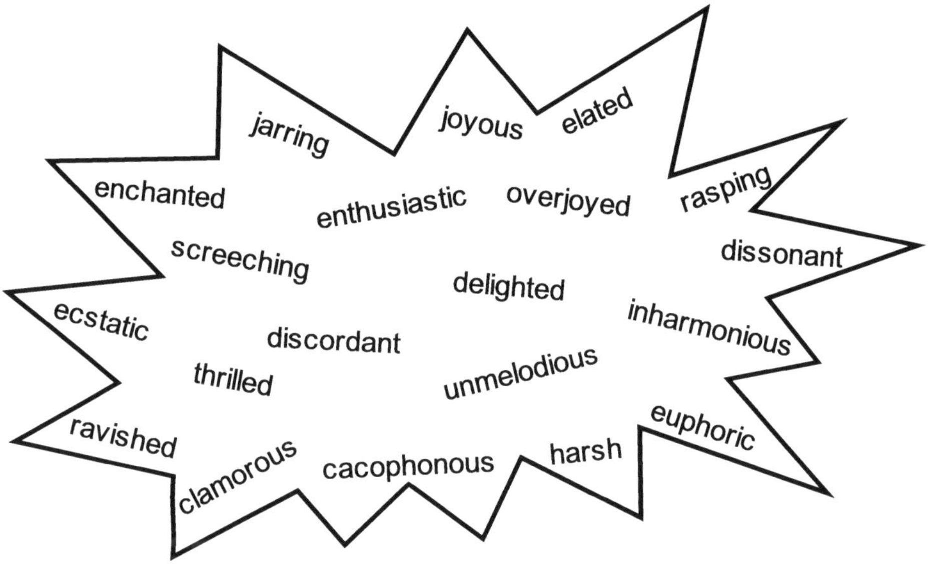

Split similar words from the bubble above into their respective columns

Rapturous	**Raucous**
1.	1.
2.	2.
3.	3.
4.	4.
5.	5.
6.	6.
7.	7.
8.	8.
9.	9.
10.	10.

41. Rebuff *verb*	42. Reinforce *verb*
reject (someone or something) in an abrupt or ungracious manner.	strengthen.

promote decline fortify
reject uphold repulse brace
support spurn boost defend
toughen ignore repudiate
repel supplement refuse
disdain enhance snub

Split similar words from the bubble above into their respective columns

Rebuff	**Reinforce**
1.	1.
2.	2.
3.	3.
4.	4.
5.	5.
6.	6.
7.	7.
8.	8.
9.	9.
10.	10.

43. Recuperate *verb*	44. Recoil *verb*
recover from illness or exertion; recover or regain (something lost or taken).	suddenly spring or flinch back in fear, horror, or disgust.

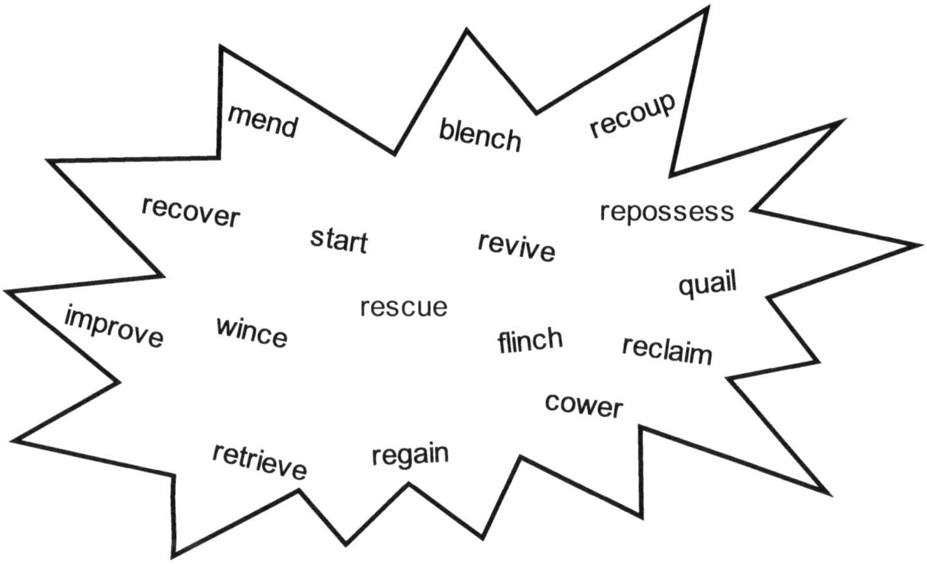

Split similar words from the bubble above into their respective columns

Recuperate	**Recoil**
1.	1.
2.	2.
3.	3.
4.	4.
5.	5.
6.	6.
7.	7.
8.	8.
9.	9.
10.	10.

45. Reckless *adjective*	**46. Redundant** *adjective* | *adjective*
heedless of danger or the consequences of one's actions; rash or impetuous.	A. not or no longer needed or useful. B. no longer in employment because there is no more work available.

imprudent
impetuous
precipitate
rash
unemployed
idle
audacious
unnecessary
inessential
unwise
thoughtless
heedless
needless
injudicious
overhasty
disposable
dismissed
jobless
discharged
superfluous

Split similar words from the bubble above into their respective columns

Reckless	**Redundant**	
1.	1.	A
2.	2.	
3.	3.	
4.	4.	
5.	5.	
6.	6.	B
7.	7.	
8.	8.	
9.	9.	
10.	10.	

47. Reconciliation *noun*	**48. Resentment** *noun*
the restoration of friendly relations.	bitter indignation at having been treated unfairly.

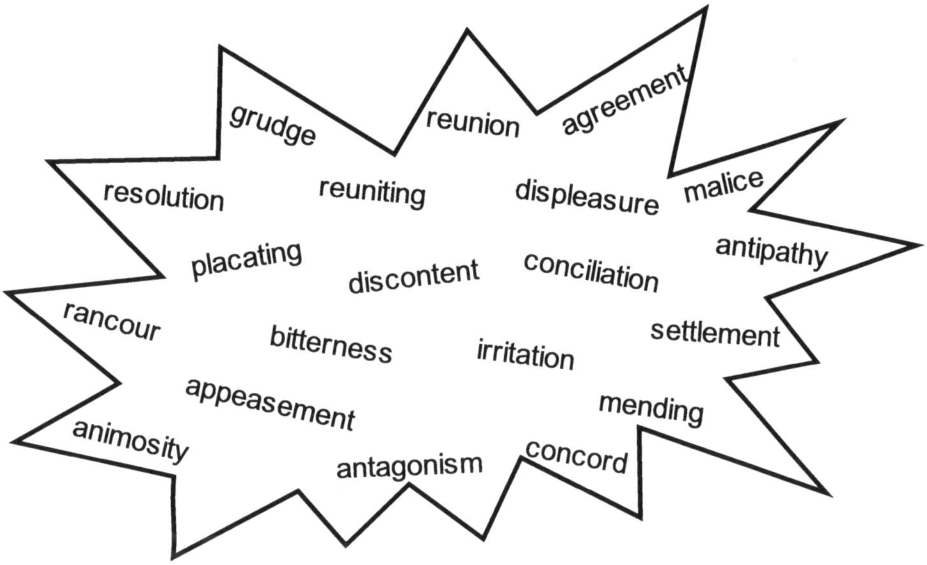

Split similar words from the bubble above into their respective columns

Reconciliation	**Resentment**
1.	1.
2.	2.
3.	3.
4.	4.
5.	5.
6.	6.
7.	7.
8.	8.
9.	9.
10.	10.

49. Rejuvenate *verb*	50. Remunerate *verb*
make (someone or something) look or feel better, younger, or more vital.	pay (someone) for services rendered or work done.

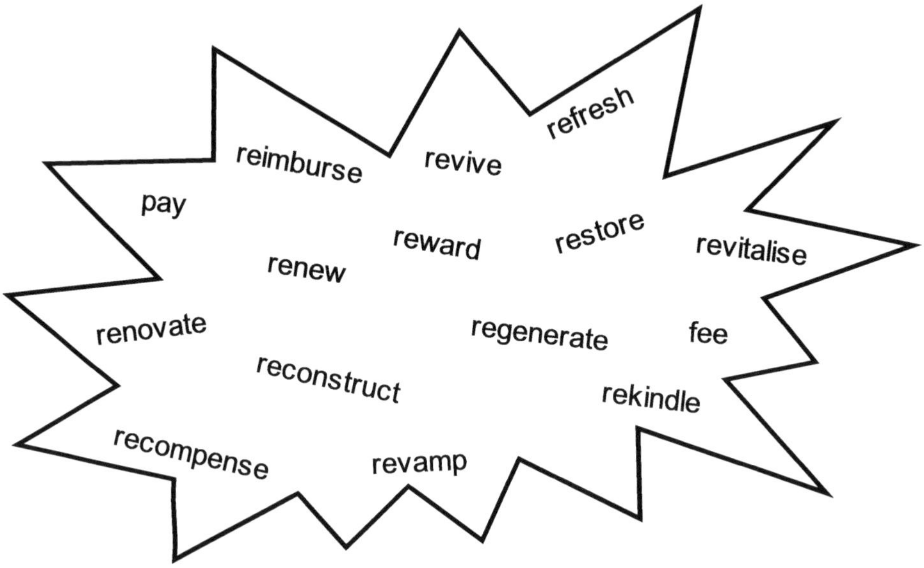

Split similar words from the bubble above into their respective columns

Rejuvenate	**Remunerate**
1.	1.
2.	2.
3.	3.
4.	4.
5.	5.
6.	6.
7.	7.
8.	8.
9.	9.
10.	10.

51. Remorseful *adjective*	52. Repulsive *adjective*
filled with deep regret or guilt.	arousing intense distaste or disgust.

repentant rueful despicable
repellent deplorable contrite obnoxious
sorry revolting regretful
abhorrent repugnant ashamed apologetic
guilty offensive
abominable penitent disgusting sad

Split similar words from the bubble above into their respective columns

Remorseful	**Repulsive**
1.	1.
2.	2.
3.	3.
4.	4.
5.	5.
6.	6.
7.	7.
8.	8.
9.	9.
10.	10.

53. Radical *adjective | (noun) adjective*	**54. Revered** *adjective*
A. relating to the essential part; thorough. B. (a person or organisation) advocating or based on total political/social change.	deeply respected or admired.

complete absolute fundamental
worshiped venerated cherished fanatic
respected quintessential extremist
honoured admired esteemed
revolutionary
appreciated valued
idolised reforming intrinsic zealot

Split similar words from the bubble above into their respective columns

Radical	**Revered**
1.	1.
2.	2.
3.	3.
4.	4.
5.	5.
6.	6.
7.	7.
8.	8.
9.	9.
10.	10.

55. Revitalise *verb*	**56. Reprimand** *(verb) noun*
imbue something with new life and vitality.	(address) a formal expression of disapproval.

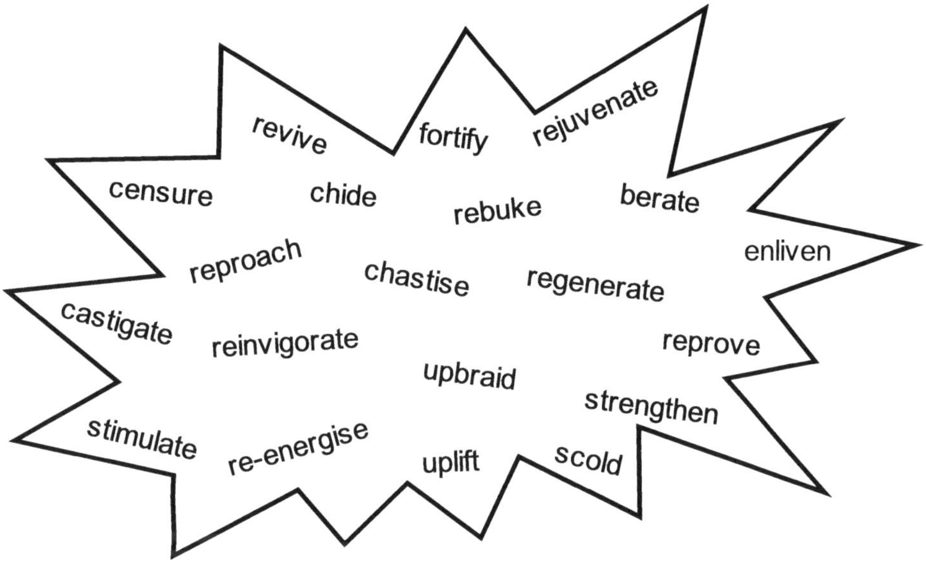

Split similar words from the bubble above into their respective columns

Revitalise	**Reprimand**
1.	1.
2.	2.
3.	3.
4.	4.
5.	5.
6.	6.
7.	7.
8.	8.
9.	9.
10.	10.

57. Roister *verb*	**58. Ruffle** *verb*
enjoy oneself or celebrate in a noisy or boisterous way.	disorder or disarrange (someone's hair), typically by running one's hands through it.

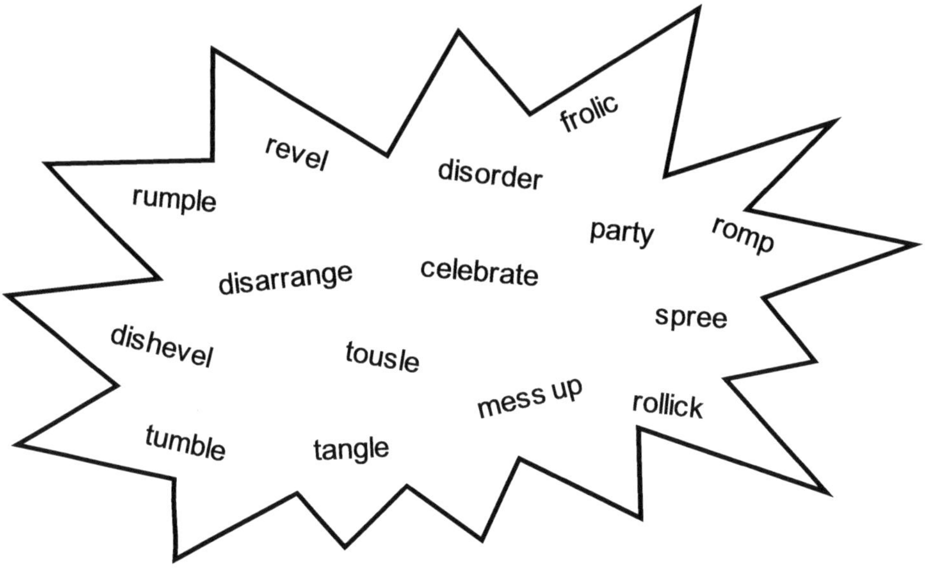

Split similar words from the bubble above into their respective columns

Roister	**Ruffle**
1.	1.
2.	2.
3.	3.
4.	4.
5.	5.
6.	6.
7.	7.
8.	8.
9.	9.
10.	10.

59. Rift *noun*	60. Rebuke *(verb) noun*
a crack, split, or break in something; a serious break in friendly relations.	(give) an expression of sharp disapproval or criticism.

criticism squabble censure
aperture upbraiding berate
fissure admonishment
conflict rollicking
scolding crevice
reproach fault
breach reprimand
quarrel reproof cranny flaw

Split similar words from the bubble above into their respective columns

Rift	Rebuke
1.	1.
2.	2.
3.	3.
4.	4.
5.	5.
6.	6.
7.	7.
8.	8.
9.	9.
10.	10.

61. Rigorous *adjective*	62. Robust *adjective*
extremely thorough and careful.	strong and healthy.

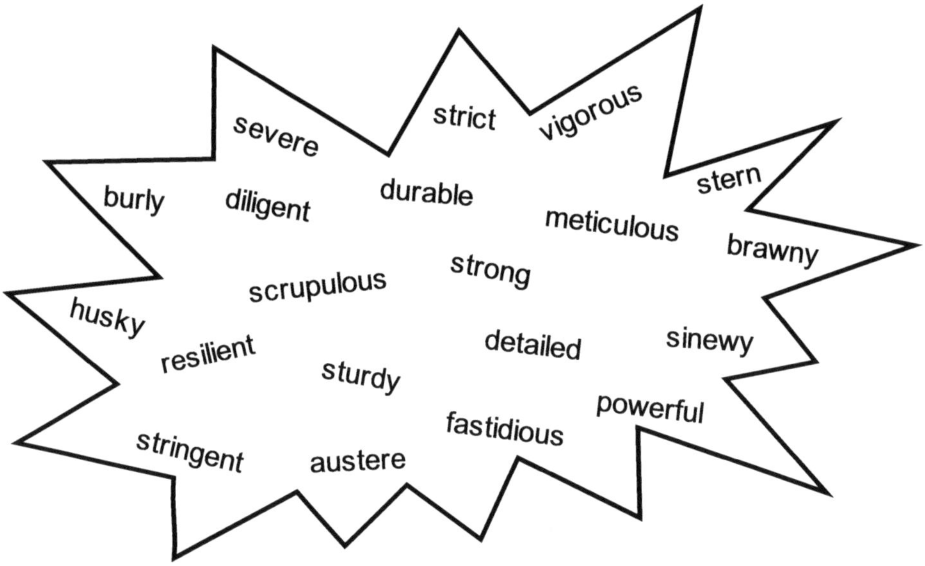

Split similar words from the bubble above into their respective columns

Rigorous	**Robust**
1.	1.
2.	2.
3.	3.
4.	4.
5.	5.
6.	6.
7.	7.
8.	8.
9.	9.
10.	10.

63. Roguish *adjective*	64. Rueful *adjective*
characteristic of a dishonest or unprincipled person; playfully mischievous.	expressing sorrow or regret, especially in a wry or humorous way.

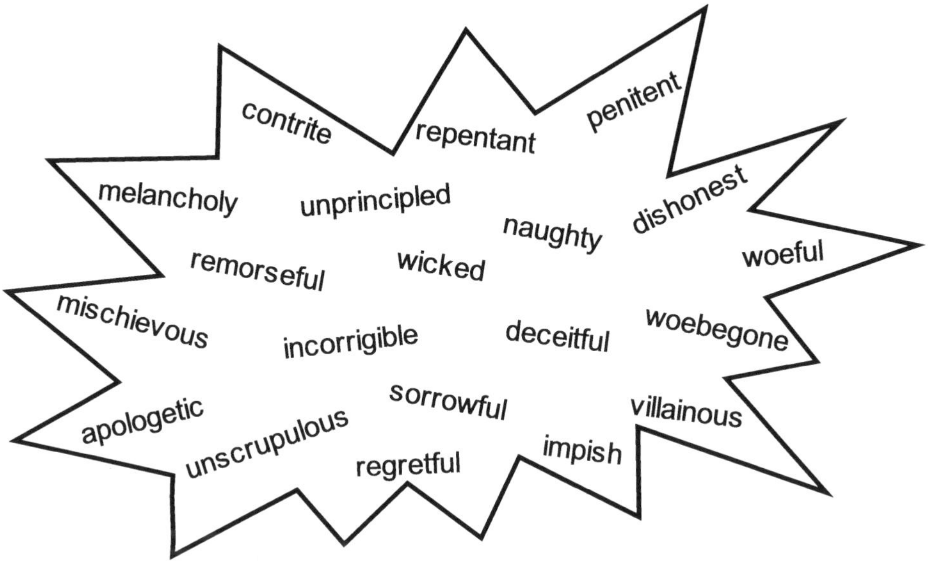

Split similar words from the bubble above into their respective columns

Roguish	Rueful
1.	1.
2.	2.
3.	3.
4.	4.
5.	5.
6.	6.
7.	7.
8.	8.
9.	9.
10.	10.

65. Rugged *adjective | adjective*	**66. Repugnant** *adjective*
A. (of ground) having a rocky surface. B. strongly made and capable of withstanding rough handling.	extremely distasteful.

uneven, obscene, rough, horrendous, abhorrent, strong, hideous, resilient, repulsive, jagged, irregular, abominable, robust, tough, gruesome, obnoxious, loathsome, durable, craggy, appalling

Split similar words from the bubble above into their respective columns

	Rugged	**Repugnant**
A	1.	1.
	2.	2.
	3.	3.
	4.	4.
	5.	5.
B	6.	6.
	7.	7.
	8.	8.
	9.	9.
	10.	10.

67. Rupture *verb & (noun)*	**68. Refute** *verb*
breach, disturb or break. (a breach of a harmonious relationship).	prove a statement or theory to be wrong or false.

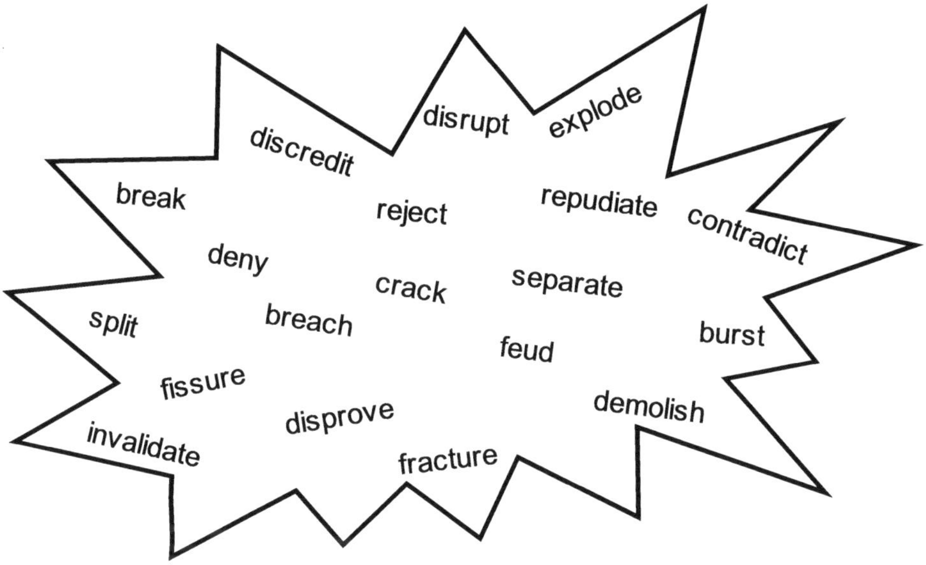

Split similar words from the bubble above into their respective columns

Rupture	Refute
1.	1.
2.	2.
3.	3.
4.	4.
5.	5.
6.	6.
7.	7.
8.	8.
9.	9.
10.	10.

69. Reprobate *adjective*	70. Ruthless *adjective*
unprincipled.	having or showing no pity or compassion for others.

callous
ferocious
merciless
incorrigible
debauched
pitiless
harsh
unprincipled
roguish
savage
shameless
wicked
immoral
relentless
brutal
corrupt
inhuman
dissipated
vicious

Split similar words from the bubble above into their respective columns

Reprobate	**Ruthless**
1.	1.
2.	2.
3.	3.
4.	4.
5.	5.
6.	6.
7.	7.
8.	8.
9.	9.
10.	10.

Synonymless Words

These are words with few or no synonyms.

Word		Definition
71.	Regal	fit for a monarch, especially in being magnificent or dignified.
72.	Rhapsody	an effusively enthusiastic or ecstatic expression of feeling.
	Rhapsody (2)	an epic poem
73.	Ramekin	a small dish for baking and serving an individual portion of food.
74.	Regime	a government, especially an authoritarian one.
75.	Referendum	a general vote by the electorate on a single political question.
76.	Regatta	a sporting event consisting of a series of boat or yacht races.
77.	Rendezvous	a meeting at an agreed time and place; a meeting place.
78.	Resin	a sticky substance that comes from plants or is manufactured used in plastics, etc.
79.	Risotto	an Italian dish of rice cooked in stock.

A Crossword for Synonymless Words can be found near the end of this book.

Answers & Revision Sheets

1. Rapt	2. Resolute	3. Rambling
• Fascinated • Charmed • Ecstatic • Rapturous • Enthralled • Captivated • Mesmerised • Enchanted • Engrossed • Spellbound	• Committed • Adamant • Purposive • Firm • Undaunted • Staunch • Stalwart • Tenacious • Obstinate • Obdurate	• Lengthy • Confused • Long winded • Prolix • Wordy • Verbose • Garrulous • Wandering • Labyrinthine • Twisting
4. Rudimentary	**5. Ramshackle**	**6. Rancid**
• Basic • Elementary • Introductory • Early • Initial • Crude • Unsophisticated • Rough • Primitive • Fundamental	• Dilapidated • Derelict • Ruinous • Decrepit • Neglected • Decaying • Disintegrating • Rickety • Run down • Crumbling	• Sour • Stale • Rotten • Revolting • Tainted • Putrid • Foul • Rank • Unpleasant • Bad
7. Recluse	**8. Renegade**	**9. Rebate**
• Monk • Nun • Ascetic • Hermit • Solitary • Introvert • Loner	• Traitor • Defector • Deserter • Turncoat • Rebel • Treacherous • Rebellious • Mutinous • Traitorous • Disloyal	• Discount • Deduction • Reduction • Decrease • Allowance • Concession • Repayment

Answers & Revision Sheets R

10. Rubble	11. Reel	12. Reproach
• Debris • Remains • Wreckage • Ruin	• Stagger • Lurch • Stumble • Waver • Swerve • Roll • Totter • Wobble • Rock	• Rebuke • Reproof • Reprimand • Admonition • Censure • Chastise • Upbraid • Berate • Castigate • Chide
13. Raze	**14. Replenish**	**15. Repudiate**
• Destroy • Demolish • Flatten • Bulldoze • Ruin • Wreck • Knock down • Wipe out	• Refill • Top up • Recharge • Reload • Freshen • Plenish • Replace • Renew • Restock • Restore	• Reject • Renounce • Abandon • Deny • Refute • Contradict • Disclaim • Disavow • Desert • Negate
16. Rave	**17. Relinquish**	**18. Recede**
• Babble • Ramble • Maunder • Rant • Extol • Eulogise • Acclaim • Festivity • Celebration • Frolic	• Give up • Resign • Abdicate • Surrender • Leave • Abandon • Kick • Forgo • Vacate • Quit	• Lessen • Fade • Abate • Ebb • Swindle • Shrink • Diminish • Dwindle • Wane • Subside

19. Revel	20. Reimburse	21. Reek
• Enjoy • Celebrate • Party • Love • Adore • Like • Roister • Relish • Feast	• Compensate • Recompense • Refund • Repay • Return • Restore • Replace	• Stink • Smell • Stench • Whiff
22. Ravage	**23. Recurrent**	**24. Reticent**
• Devastate • Destroy • Raze • Demolish • Wreck • Plunder • Ransack • Pillage • Harry • Maraud	• Repeated • Cyclic • Cyclical • Perennial • Habitual • Chronic • Frequent • Sporadic • Spasmodic • Intermittent	• Shy • Reserved • Introverted • Diffident • Withdrawn • Modest • Secretive • Quiet • Uncommunicative • Taciturn
25. Rife	**26. Reclusive**	**27. Rile**
• Widespread • Universal • Ubiquitous • Global • Prevalent • Alive • Insidious • Pervading • Overflowing • Bursting	• Solitary • Secluded • Isolated • Cloistered • Retiring • Introverted • Sequestered • Hermit-like • Unsociable • Antisocial	• Provoke • Anger • Affront • Infuriate • Exasperate • Vex • Aggravate • Irritate • Bother • Irk

Answers & Revision Sheets R

28. Revile	29. Retort	30. Relish
• Criticise • Condemn • Attack • Abuse • Censure • Denounce • Defame • Slander • Malign • Smear	• Answer • Reply • Respond • Return • Counter • Rejoin • Riposte • Retaliate • Acknowledge • Comeback	• Enjoy • Savour • Rapture • Exhilaration • Zest • Sauce • Condiment • Accompaniment • Dressing • Flavouring
31. Ragged	**32. Ravishing**	**33. Raiment**
• Tattered • Torn • Split • Frayed • Scruffy • Shabby • Rugged • Craggy • Uneven • Rough	• Gorgeous • Stunning • Wonderful • Exquisite • Dazzling • Radiant • Enchanting • Fabulous • Magnificent • Divine	• Apparel • Clothes • Clothing • Garments • Attire • Dress • Costume • Garb • Outfit • Vestment
34. Rapport	**35. Rancour**	**36. Recess**
• Affinity • Bond • Empathy • Harmony • Sympathy • Link • Accord	• Bitterness • Spite • Hate • Resentment • Malice • Hatred • Hostility • Animosity • Malevolence • Antipathy	• Cavity • Cranny • Hole • Nook • Indentation • Hiatus • Interlude • Intermission • Halt • Lull

37. Ransack	38. Rasp	39. Rapturous
• Plunder • Pillage • Raid • Rob • Loot • Maraud • Ravage • Devastate • Steal	• Scrape • Rub • Abrade • Grate • Scratch • Scour • File • Grind	• Ecstatic • Joyous • Elated • Euphoric • Enchanted • Delighted • Thrilled • Overjoyed • Enthusiastic • Ravished
40. Raucous	**41. Rebuff**	**42. Reinforce**
• Harsh • Screeching • Discordant • Dissonant • Inharmonious • Unmelodious • Jarring • Rasping • Clamorous • Cacophonous	• Reject • Spurn • Refuse • Repel • Repudiate • Repulse • Snub • Disdain • Decline • Ignore	• Fortify • Brace • Toughen • Support • Uphold • Defend • Boost • Promote • Supplement • Enhance
43. Recuperate	**44. Recoil**	**45. Reckless**
• Improve • Mend • Revive • Regain • Recoup • Retrieve • Recover • Reclaim • Repossess • Rescue	• Flinch • Blench • Start • Wince • Cower • Quail	• Rash • Thoughtless • Overhasty • Impetuous • Precipitate • Audacious • Injudicious • Imprudent • Unwise • Heedless

Answers & Revision Sheets R

46. Redundant

- Unnecessary
- Inessential
- Needless
- Disposable
- Superfluous

- Dismissed
- Discharged
- Unemployed
- Idle
- Jobless

47. Reconciliation

- Reuniting
- Reunion
- Conciliation
- Appeasement
- Placating
- Resolution
- Settlement
- Mending
- Concord
- Agreement

48. Resentment

- Bitterness
- Irritation
- Displeasure
- Discontent
- Rancour
- Animosity
- Antagonism
- Antipathy
- Malice
- Grudge

49. Rejuvenate

- Revive
- Revitalise
- Renew
- Regenerate
- Restore
- Refresh
- Reconstruct
- Renovate
- Rekindle
- Revamp

50. Remunerate

- Pay
- Reward
- Reimburse
- Recompense
- Fee

51. Remorseful

- Sorry
- Regretful
- Sad
- Contrite
- Repentant
- Guilty
- Ashamed
- Rueful
- Apologetic
- Penitent

52. Repulsive

- Revolting
- Disgusting
- Abhorrent
- Repellent
- Repugnant
- Offensive
- Deplorable
- Despicable
- Obnoxious
- Abominable

53. Radical

- Complete
- Absolute
- Fundamental
- Quintessential
- Intrinsic

- Revolutionary
- Reforming
- Zealot
- Extremist
- Fanatic

54. Revered

- Respected
- Admired
- Esteemed
- Cherished
- Worshiped
- Venerated
- Appreciated
- Idolised
- Honoured
- Valued

Answers & Revision Sheets R

55. Revitalise

- Reinvigorate
- Re-energise
- Strengthen
- Regenerate
- Fortify
- Revive
- Rejuvenate
- Enliven
- Uplift
- Stimulate

56. Reprimand

- Chide
- Chastise
- Upbraid
- Castigate
- Censure
- Berate
- Reprove
- Rebuke
- Reproach
- Scold

57. Roister

- Celebrate
- Romp
- Party
- Spree
- Rollick
- Revel
- Frolic

58. Ruffle

- Disarrange
- Tousle
- Dishevel
- Rumple
- Disorder
- Mess up
- Tangle
- Tumble

59. Rift

- Aperture
- Fault
- Flaw
- Breach
- Quarrel
- Squabble
- Conflict
- Cranny
- Fissure
- Crevice

60. Rebuke

- Reprimand
- Scolding
- Admonishment
- Upbraiding
- Criticism
- Reproach
- Reproof
- Censure
- Berate
- Rollicking

61. Rigorous

- Meticulous
- Diligent
- Scrupulous
- Detailed
- Fastidious
- Stringent
- Austere
- Strict
- Severe
- Stern

62. Robust

- Strong
- Sturdy
- Powerful
- Resilient
- Durable
- Vigorous
- Brawny
- Burly
- Husky
- Sinewy

63. Roguish

- Unprincipled
- Dishonest
- Wicked
- Villainous
- Deceitful
- Unscrupulous
- Impish
- Mischievous
- Naughty
- Incorrigible

Answers & Revision Sheets <u>R</u>

64. Rueful	65. Rugged	66. Repugnant
• Sorrowful • Regretful • Apologetic • Remorseful • Contrite • Repentant • Penitent • Woeful • Woebegone • Melancholy	• Rough • Uneven • Jagged • Irregular • Craggy • Durable • Robust • Tough • Resilient • Strong	• Abhorrent • Repulsive • Loathsome • Abominable • Gruesome • Horrendous • Obnoxious • Appalling • Hideous • Obscene
67. Rupture	**68. Refute**	**69. Reprobate**
• Crack • Burst • Fissure • Fracture • Break • Disrupt • Separate • Breach • Split • Feud	• Deny • Reject • Demolish • Disprove • Repudiate • Explode • Contradict • Invalidate • Discredit	• Roguish • Wicked • Unprincipled • Shameless • Immoral • Dissipated • Corrupt • Incorrigible • Debauched
70. Ruthless		
• Merciless • Pitiless • Harsh • Callous • Relentless • Brutal • Inhuman • Savage • Vicious • Ferocious		

Test Yourself: R

Fill in the gaps! This will help refresh your memory of all the words you have just covered. The first one is done for you.

1. Fascinated	R A P T
2. Uplift	R _ V _ _ A L _ S _
3. Reject	R _ P _ D _ _ T _
4. Wreckage	R _ B B _ _
5. Basic	R _ D _ M _ _ T _ _ Y
6. Disarrange	R _ F F _ _
7. Destroy	R _ V _ _ E
8. Improve	R _ C _ P _ R _ _ E
9. Solitary	R _ C _ _ S _
10. Detailed	R _ G _ R _ U _
11. Widespread	R _ F _
12. Ramble/Praise/Celebration	R _ V _
13. Needless/Unemployed	R _ D _ _ D _ _ T
14. Defame	R _ V _ _ E

15. Committed	R _ S _ L _ T _
16. Scold	R _ P _ _ M _ _ D
17. Refund	R _ _ M B _ _ S _
18. Stumble	R _ _ L
19. Decaying	R _ _ S _ A C _ _ E
20. Breach/Quarrel	R _ F _
21. Repeated	R _ C _ R R _ _ T
22. Refill	R _ P _ _ N _ S _
23. Rebel/Disloyal	R _ N E _ _ D _
24. Strong	R _ B _ S _
25. Isolated	R _ C _ U _ _ V _
26. Give up	R _ _ I N _ U _ S _
27. Reunion	R _ C _ N C _ L _ _ T _ _ N
28. Respond	R _ T _ _ T
29. Scrape	R _ S _

30. Loot	R _ N _ A _ K
31. Lengthy	R _ M _ _ I N _
32. Celebrate	R _ _ S _ E _
33. Stink	R _ _ K
34. Scold	R _ P _ O A _ H
35. Rotten	R _ N _ I D
36. Criticism	R _ B _ K _
37. Shy	R _ T _ C _ _ T
38. Celebrate	R _ V _ L
39. Discount	R _ _ A _ E
40. Dishonest	R _ G _ _ S H
41. Irritate	R _ L _
42. Lessen	R _ C _ _ E
43. Bitterness	R _ _ E N _ M _ _ T
44. Enjoy/Accompaniment	R _ _ I S H

45. Hole/Intermission R _ C _ S S

46. Apologetic R _ E _ U _

47. Refresh R _ J _ V _ _ A _ E

48. Torn R _ G G _ _

49. Unmelodious R _ U C _ _ S

50. Crack R _ P _ _ R _

51. Disgusting R _ P U _ S _ V _

52. Bond R _ P P _ _ T

53. Destroy R _ Z _

54. Merciless R _ T _ L _ S S

55. Thoughtless R _ _ K _ E _ _

56. Rough/Strong R _ G G _ _

57. Pay R _ M _ N _ R _ _ E

58. Wonderful R _ V _ S H _ _ G

59. Decline R _ B _ F F

60. Deny R _ F _ T _

61. Absolute/Revolutionary R _ D _ C _ _

62. Hatred R _ N _ _ U R

63. Flinch R _ C _ _ L

64. Thrilled R _ P _ U _ _ U _

65. Horrendous R _ P _ G _ _ N T

66. Sorry R _ M _ _ S E _ _ L

67. Clothing R _ I _ E _ T

68. Support R _ I _ _ O R _ E

69. Shameless R _ P _ _ B _ _ E

70. Respected R _ V _ R _ D

Please turn over for Answers

Answers

1. Rapt
2. Revitalise
3. Repudiate
4. Rubble
5. Rudimentary
6. Ruffle
7. Ravage
8. Recuperate
9. Recluse
10. Rigorous
11. Rife
12. Rave
13. Redundant
14. Revile
15. Resolute
16. Reprimand
17. Reimburse
18. Reel
19. Ramshackle
20. Rift
21. Recurrent
22. Replenish
23. Renegade
24. Robust
25. Reclusive
26. Relinquish
27. Reconciliation
28. Retort
29. Rasp
30. Ransack
31. Rambling
32. Roister
33. Reek
34. Reproach
35. Rancid
36. Rebuke
37. Reticent
38. Revel
39. Rebate
40. Roguish
41. Rile
42. Recede
43. Resentment
44. Relish
45. Recess
46. Rueful
47. Rejuvenate
48. Ragged
49. Raucous
50. Rupture
51. Repulsive
52. Rapport
53. Raze
54. Ruthless
55. Reckless
56. Rugged
57. Remunerate
58. Ravishing
59. Rebuff
60. Refute
61. Radical
62. Rancour
63. Recoil
64. Rapturous
65. Repugnant
66. Remorseful
67. Raiment
68. Reinforce
69. Reprobate
70. Revered

Synonymless Words Crossword: Q – R

Across
3. fit for a monarch.
5. a meeting or meeting place.
6. an enthusiastic feeling; an epic poem.
9. a general vote by electorate.
10. a sticky substance used in plastics.
11. a hard pear-shaped fruit.

Down
1. a government.
2. a hard prism-shaped mineral.
4. a favour in exchange for something.
5. an Italian dish.
6. a small dish for baking.
7. a boat racing event.
8. a baked flan or tart.

Word Bank

Q

1. Quintessential
2. Quaint
3. Quay
4. Quandary
5. Quell
6. Quail

Synonymless words

7. Quiche
8. Quid pro quo
9. Quince
10. Quartz

R

1. Rapt
2. Resolute
3. Rambling
4. Rudimentary
5. Ramshackle
6. Rancid
7. Recluse
8. Renegade
9. Rebate
10. Rubble
11. Reel
12. Reproach
13. Recuperate
14. Replenish
15. Revel
16. Rave
17. Relinquish
18. Recede
19. Repudiate
20. Reimburse
21. Reek
22. Ravage
23. Recurrent
24. Reticent
25. Rife
26. Reclusive
27. Rile
28. Revile
29. Retort
30. Relish
31. Ragged
32. Ravishing
33. Raiment
34. Rapport
35. Rancour
36. Recess
37. Ransack
38. Rasp
39. Rapturous
40. Raucous
41. Rebuff
42. Reinforce
43. Raze
44. Recoil
45. Reckless
46. Redundant
47. Reconciliation
48. Resentment
49. Rejuvenate
50. Remunerate
51. Remorseful
52. Repulsive
53. Radical
54. Revered
55. Revitalise
56. Reprimand
57. Roister
58. Ruffle
59. Rift
60. Rebuke
61. Rigorous
62. Robust
63. Roguish
64. Rueful
65. Rugged
66. Repugnant
67. Rupture
68. Refute
69. Reprobate
70. Ruthless

Synonymless words

71. Regal
72. Rhapsody
73. Ramekin
74. Regime
75. Referendum
76. Regatta
77. Rendezvous
78. Resin
79. Risotto

Crossword Answers

Congratulations!

In this book you have added 89 words to your word bank.

This brings you total A - R word bank to **1004 advanced words**!

Printed in Great Britain
by Amazon

48352033R00041